RECIPES
---- for ----
DISASTER

Edited by Pam Sommers

CHRONICLE BOOKS
SAN FRANCISCO

DEDICATION

To Peter, for a dozen years of love, patience, and humor

Acknowledgments

Thanks to every artist who found time in a loaded schedule to make a dish for this party,
a perfect example of the generosity of spirit and support that has sustained us from Day One.

Thanks to Bill LeBlond, my editor, and everyone else at Chronicle Books who liked this
unique project and believed in it enough to publish it.

Thanks, finally, to my sister Florie for helping me organize the paper trail.

Special thanks to S.G. for seeing the possibilities in everything and sharing them with us.

Collection Copyright © 1993 Pam Sommers.

Library of Congress Cataloging-in-Publication Data
Recipes for disaster : dinner at the Illustration Gallery / edited by Pam Sommers
p. cm.
ISBN 0-8118-0299-X
1. Cookery—Caricatures and cartoons. 2. American wit and humor, Pictorial. 3. Cookery.
I. Sommers, Pam. II. Illustration Gallery.
NC1426.R33 1993
741.5'973—dc20
92-30866
CIP

Printed in United States of America Distributed in Canada by Raincoast Books,
112 East Third Ave., Vancouver, B.C. V5T 1C8

10 9 8 7 6 5 4 3 2 1

Chronicle Books
275 Fifth Street
San Francisco, CA 94103

INTERIOR DESIGN BY WENDY KASSNER

CONTENTS

- - - - - - -

INTRODUCTION

THE ILLUSTRATION GALLERY, which opened on December 1, 1988, is the only gallery in the United States devoted exclusively to showing contemporary illustration. We opened with a group show featuring the work of fifteen artists and since that time have had the pleasure of providing a venue for the work of well over one hundred different illustrators.

In August of 1990, while working on an exhibition of food and wine illustration called The Artist's Palate, I was struck with the idea of doing a cookbook. I personally love cooking and, obviously, illustration, so it seemed like an ideal marriage.

With just three months before the show, I wasted no time in calling up an initial group of illustrators to see how the idea would go over. Luckily, my enthusiasm was returned, and in short order, forty-one artists committed to doing a piece for the book.

The only compensation was complete freedom to do whatever they wanted, as long as it could in some way be considered a "recipe" for something. Illustrators, almost by definition, translate existing material (a book, an article, an event) into a visual form. However, they are hardly ever given free rein to do just what they please and these opportunities are highly prized. This book, containing the work of eighty-four artists, is simply an expanded version of that early limited-edition effort.

Many artists chose to do a real recipe, but an equal number took a conceptual departure resulting, for example, in "recipes" for a riot, a proper bath, and stainless steel. I think you will agree that many of the recipes sound wonderful. Nevertheless, it is up to the reader to decide for him or herself which ones are the real recipes and which should be taken with an added "grain of salt"—if not avoided entirely—at least in the kitchen!

I hope you enjoy *Recipes for Disaster* as much as I enjoyed editing it. Bon Appetit!

Protestant Pasta

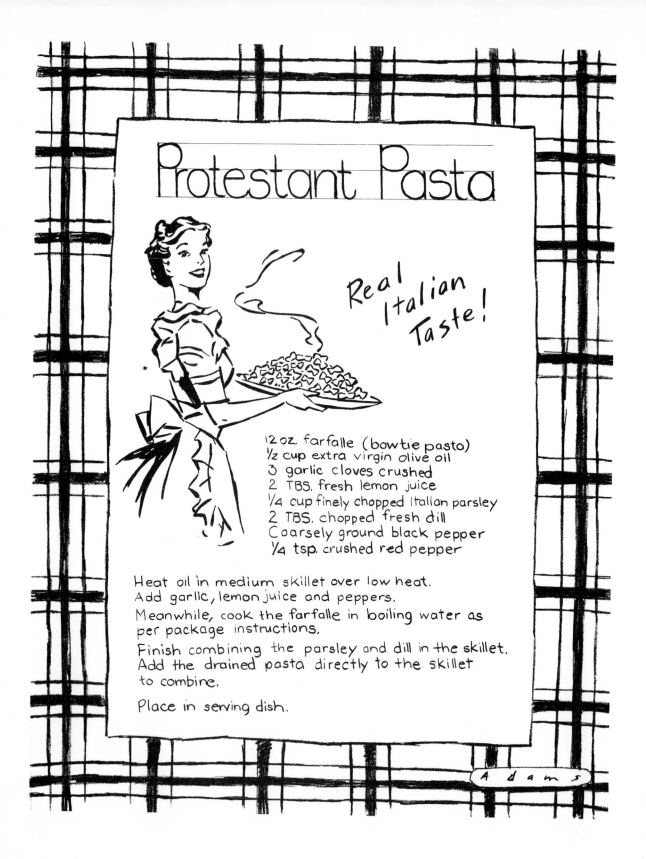

Real Italian Taste!

12 oz. farfalle (bowtie pasta)
½ cup extra virgin olive oil
3 garlic cloves crushed
2 TBS. fresh lemon juice
¼ cup finely chopped Italian parsley
2 TBS. chopped fresh dill
Coarsely ground black pepper
¼ tsp. crushed red pepper

Heat oil in medium skillet over low heat.
Add garlic, lemon juice and peppers.

Meanwhile, cook the farfalle in boiling water as per package instructions.

Finish combining the parsley and dill in the skillet.
Add the drained pasta directly to the skillet to combine.

Place in serving dish.

Adams

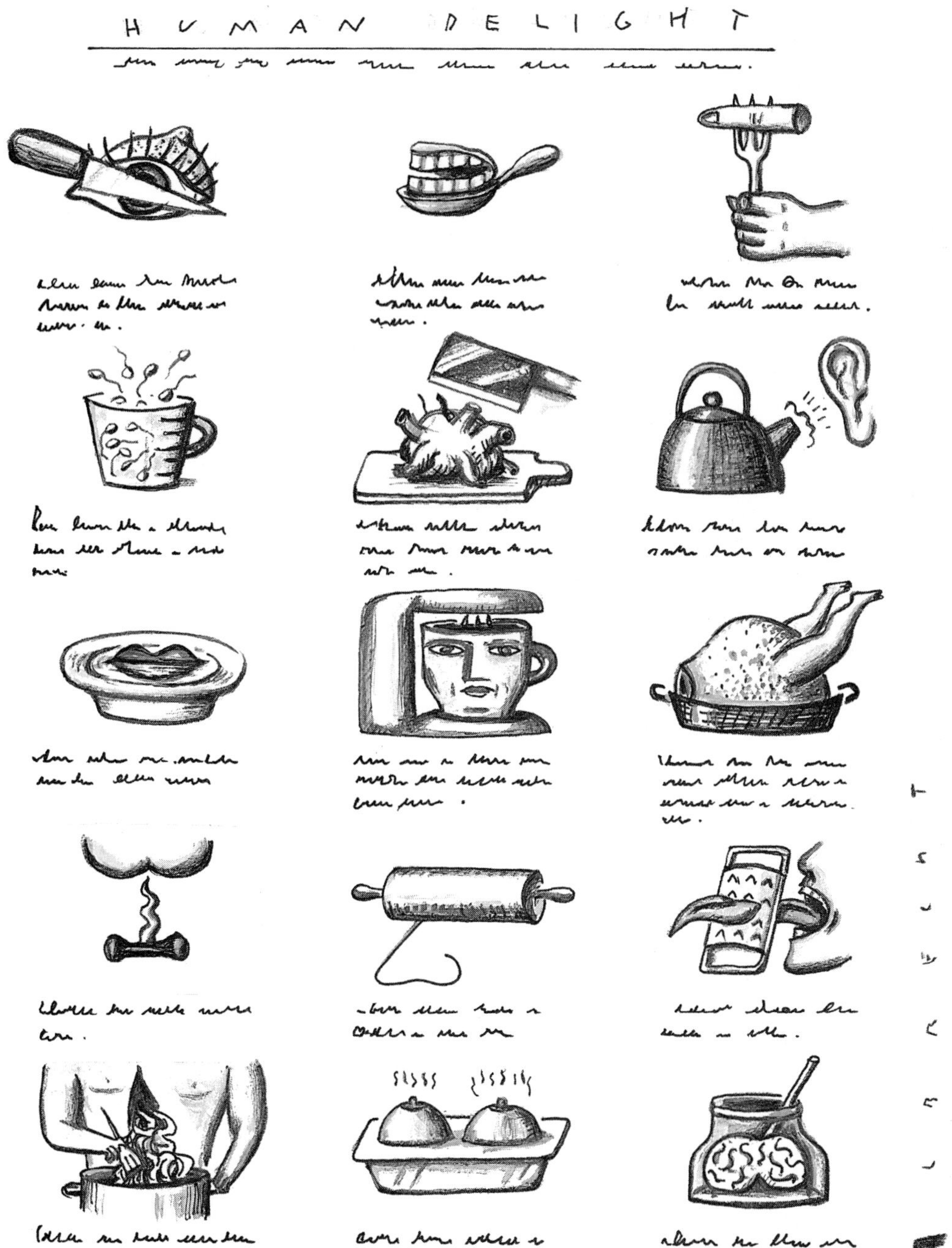
HUMAN DELIGHT

recipe for Romance

A Sprinkling of Stardust

A Dash of Candlelight

Plenty of Red Velvet

Loungewear to taste

A little Steve & Eydie

Mix well and Breathe Deeply!

Abalone COOKED IN
tin foil on the BBQ

FOR EACh
Fresh abalone :
2 tablespoons
butter
— Garlic, minced &
chopped FINE
Lemons or Lime

BEAt abalone with Wood
hAMMER on all sides. Slice
like a Loaf OF FRENCH BREAD
(Not entirely THROUGH)
Put garlic mixed in
butter betWEEN the
WEDGES. SQUEEZE
Lemon AIL OUER.
cut Lemon & Put
slices all around.
WRAP in foil.
cook on EACh side
until it
suits your
taste.

BARBOUR

A Nice Thing On A Sunday Afternoon:

French Bread
Bleu Cheese
Sweet Butter
and Wine

2 Exotic Drinx From Thailand!

Direct From Koh Samui · By M. Bartalos 1990

Tropical Itch

MIX WELL WITH CRACKED ICE: 3/4 OZ. LIGHT RUM, 3/4 OZ. DARK RUM, 1/2 OZ. ORANGE CURACAO, 3/4 OZ. GRENADINE SYRUP, 2 OZ. PINEAPPLE JUICE, 2 OZ. ORANGE JUICE, 1½ OZ. SWEET + SOUR MIX, 1 DASH ANGOSTURA BITTER. POUR INTO WOO DO GLASS.

GarNISH WITH PINEAPPLE SLICE, LEMON SLICE, CHERRY, ORCHIDS, FUNNY OBJECTS, STRAWS.

Rainbow

BRANDY →
COINTREAU →
CAMPARI →
GALLIANO →
WHITE CREME DE MENTHE →
GREEN CREME DE MENTHE →
KAHLUA →
SUGAR SYRUP →
GRENADINE SYRUP →

POUR INTO A CHILLED DELMONICO GLASS these INGREDIENTS ONE BY ONE, 1/4 OZ. EACH. POUR SLOWLY AS NOT TO MIX WITH EACH OTHER. SET BRANDY AFLAME!

Apple & Cheese Pie

Filling:

2½ lbs. Granny Smiths apples
¾ cup sugar
3 tblsp. all purpose flour
¾ tsp. ground cinnamon
¼ tsp. freshly grated nutmeg
¼ tsp. salt

Pastry:

2 cups all purpose flour
½ tsp. salt
1 cup grated old cheddar
6 tblsp. shortening
6 tblsp. chilled butter
5 to 6 tblsp. ice water

Pastry

Combine flour & salt. Add cheese & mix with a fork. Using a pastry blender cut in shortening & butter until mixture resembles coarse cornmeal. Sprinkle ice water, 1 tblsp. at a time, until dough holds together. Divide in two & wrap in wax paper. Chill for an hour.

Filling

1. Position rack in centre of oven & preheat to 425°F. On a lightly floured surface roll out one-half of the pastry. Place in a 9-inch pie pan & refrigerate.
2. Peel & core apples, then cut into ½ inch wedges. In a large bowl combine sugar, flour, cinnamon, nutmeg & salt; add the apples & toss. Add lemon juice. Turn apple filling into pastry-lined pan.
3. On lightly floured surface, roll out remaining piece of pastry to a 12-inch round. Moisten edge of bottom crust with cold water. Place top pastry over the apples & press two crusts together. Roll overhanging pastry under all around. Flute with fingertips or crimp with a fork. Cut three or four vents in the centre with a knife.
4. Brush top lightly with milk. Bake for 20 minutes; reduce the oven to 350°F & bake 20 to 30 minutes longer.

jamie bennett

FRENCH RECIPE FOR FINDING TRUFFLES.

Guy Billout

This is Easy

preheat oven to 325°

IN Roaster pan line bottom with 1 16 oz. can drained Sauerkraut. Next Lay in pork chops, kielbasa, onions, and Potatoes. Now spread Other can of Sauerkraut on top but do not drain this can. ADD Fennel seeds, just sprinkle about 2 or 1 Tbs. and 2 Tbs. of brown sugar on top. Now →

and good on a cold day

Serves 4, 5, or 6

put in oven

Takes 2 hours to cook.

Tick Tick Tick Tick

Serve with a good red wine for a good good time

any roaster pan

The dog loved it!

Ingredients

Thanks for the recipe mom.

Mary Lynn Blasutta

2 16 oz cans Sauerkraut

3 onions or NONE

5 pork chops country style remove some fat.

5 potatoes quartered

Kielbasa 12" or 16" chop to 3"

Fennel seeds

Brown Sugar

it will warm your bones

MOISHA'S HALF-BAKED POTATO

Cut a potato in half.

Bake it.

A nice crust forms on the
top-- and baking takes
half the time!

R.O. Blechman

Cathie Bleck

MISS
PUMPKIN SHOW
PUMPKIN PIE

1 lb CAN PUMPKIN
½ C BROWN SUGAR
½ tsp SALT
1 tsp GROUND CINNAMON
½ tsp GINGER
½ tsp GROUND NUTMEG
3 EGGS
⅔ C EVAPORATED MILK
¾ C MILK
1 UNBAKED PIE SHELL

COMBINE PUMPKIN
& SPICES BEAT IN
EGGS. STIR IN MILK,
MIX WELL, POUR INTO
PIE SHELL, BAKE AT
425° FOR 15 MINUTES
THEN 350° FOR 45
MINUTES UNTIL KNIFE
INSERTED IN THE
MIDDLE COMES OUT
CLEAN. COOL, SERVE
WITH WHIPPED CREAM

Susan Blubaugh

20

1   Tablespoon
1   Serving bowl
½   Box saltine crackers
1   Quart milk
Mix and share with the creatures.
Turn on "I got friends in low places".
When the Woman comes home from work
wash the spoon and bowl and fix some for her.

George Booth.

LATE OCTOBER 3. 1990

recipe for an entertaining evening

DACRON THE BARBARIAN

SEARING SALSA...

4 MEDIUM TOMATOES, SEEDED & DICED
2 JALAPENO PEPPERS, CHOPPED FINE, NO SEEDS
1/2 LEMON & 1/2 LIME, SQUEEEZED
1 TEASPOON FRESH CORIANDER, MINCED
1 MEDIUM ONION, CHOPPED

MIX, CHILL & SERVE WITH BLUE CORN CHIPS, CARROT & CUCUMBER STRIPS

Diana Bryan

VARIOUS BUNS

PLAIN BUN
FLOUR, BAKING SODA, BUTTER

BLACK BUN

FLOUR, BAKING SODA, BUTTER, INDIA INK

★ BRUSH WITH EGG FOR A GLOSSIER BUN

GIFT BUN

FOLLOW BASIC BUN RECIPE. ALLOW TO COOL.

DECORATE WITH RIBBON

HALF·A·BUN

FOLLOW BASIC BUN RECIPE. ALLOW TO COOL. CUT WITH SHARP KNIFE

POLKA·DOT BUN

FLOUR, BAKING SODA, BUTTER, MARBLES

SUNSHINE BUN

FLOUR, BAKING SODA, BUTTER, RADIUM

FUZZY BUN

FLOUR, BAKING SODA, BUTTER, HAIR TRIMMINGS

RUNNY BUN

FLOUR, BAKING SODA, BUTTER, WATER, VEGETABLE OIL

★ MAKES A LOOSER BUN

FLOUR-FREE BUN

SAWDUST POWDER, TOOTHPASTE, BAKING POWDER

KRUNCHY BUN

FOLLOW BASIC BUN RECIPE. ADD FAVORITE UNCOOKED MACARONI PRODUCT

FOR YOUR RECIPE BOX

Complete Jerk Chicken

Invite ten people over for dinner. Forget to defrost chicken.

Unbelievable Jerk Chicken

On a whim, stuff a chicken with miniature marshmallows.

Major Jerk Chicken

Cut up a chicken into tiny pieces and try to cook it in your toaster.

World's Biggest Jerk Chicken

Buy a chicken at the butcher. On your way home, leave it at the dry cleaner.

EVE'S BAKED APPLES

Preheat oven to 350°. Core apples and fill
with 1 tsp. butter, 4 tbs. milk. Sprinkle with cinnamon.
Bake for 1 hour or until soft.

Eve Chwast

TURKEY SANDWICH

2 large slices of cooked TURKEY,
a bit of Stuffing — Cranberry sauce
2 Slices of SWISS cheese. Cracked
pepper —— on TWO (2) slices of RYE
or Pumpernickel Bread (No White Bread) —
add equal amounts of Ketchup and MAYO on
both insides of Bread (2 slices of Tomato in season).

Alan E Cober

Alan Cober

27

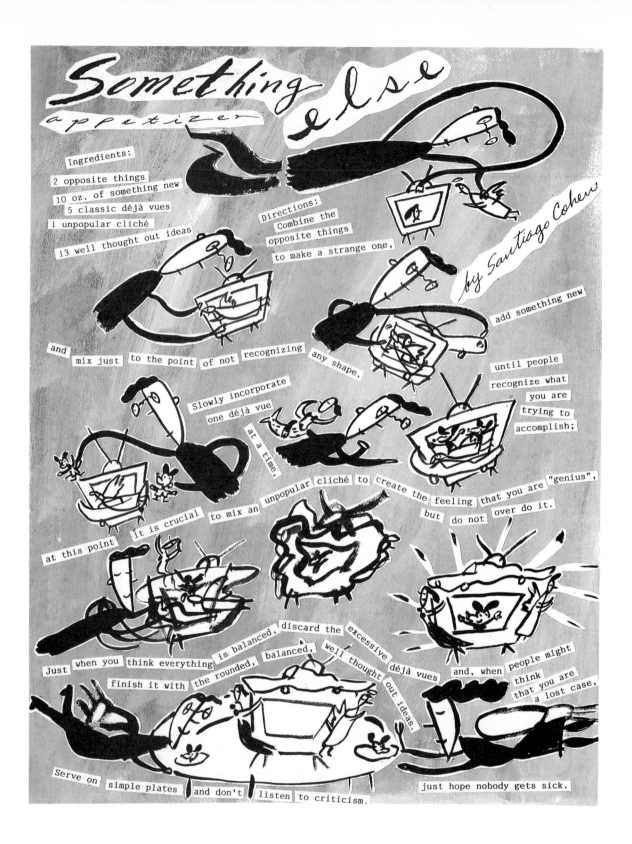

Something else

appetizer

by Santiago Cohen

Ingredients:

2 opposite things
10 oz. of something new
5 classic déjà vues
1 unpopular cliché
13 well thought out ideas

Directions:
Combine the opposite things to make a strange one, and mix just to the point of not recognizing any shape. add something new until people recognize what you are trying to accomplish; Slowly incorporate one déjà vue at a time. at this point it is crucial to mix an unpopular cliché to create the feeling that you are "genius", but do not over do it. Just when you think everything is balanced, discard the excessive déjà vues and, when people might think that you are a lost case, finish it with the rounded, balanced, well thought out ideas. Serve on simple plates and don't listen to criticism. just hope nobody gets sick.

Santiago Cohen

28

HEY GANG!! HERE'S PAUL CORIO'S ~~QUICK~~ ~~EASY~~ ~~PAINLESS~~ ~~FAMOUS~~ RECIPE FOR A

SQUANDERED YOUTH

DIRECTIONS: PUT ON SUIT. MIX GIRLS, DRINKS, SMOKES, PHARMACEUTICALS AND DICE. ADD ASPIRIN AS NECESSARY. LET SIMMER FOR FIFTEEN YEARS. LOOK BACK REGRETFULLY.

O.K., LET'S GET STARTED!! HERE ARE THE INGREDIENTS YOU'LL NEED:

DRINKS

DICE

SHOWGIRLS

ASPIRINS

SMOKES

PHARMACEUTICALS

A SHARP SUIT

©1992 PAUL CORIO

MAY ELEVENTH 1992

SHOE POLISHING

IF NECESSARY REMOVE ANY SURFACE DUST USING A CLOTH. THEN APPLY POLISH WITH A BRUSH OR DUSTER.

WORK THE POLISH WELL INTO THE SHOE. FOR A BRILLIANT SHINE BUFF BRISKLY WITH A SOFT BRUSH OR A DUSTER. POLISHING SHOES DAILY CAN PROLONG THE LIFE OF YOUR SHOES.

la Brioche

in 10 easy steps

isabelle Dervaux

1 Mix 2 cups of Milk + 2 sticks of butter + 1/4 cup of sugar. Let it cool in a big bowl.

2 Add 2 packages of active dry yeast - wait 10 mm.

3 Beat 3 eggs (room temp.) + 3 tblspoons of salt + 7 cups of sifted Flour (one at a time)

4 Floor a work surface. the dough becomes elastic

5 Knead the dough about 10 mm. Pour 2 tblspoons of veg oil unto the bowl. Put in the dough.

6 Set dough on a WARM place. Cover up with a towel it should triple in about 3 hrs.

7 Punch the dough down again on a flour surface for 2mm Return to bowl.

8 Let it rise again Cover it -

9 Bake for 30 to 40 mm.

10 Unmold after the brioche has cooled.

Et voilà!

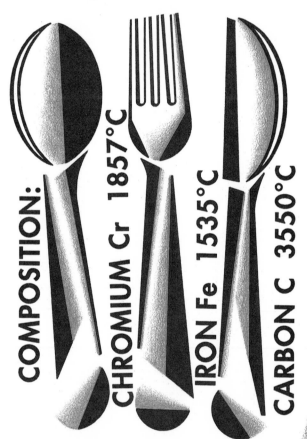

STAINLESS STEEL

COMPOSITION:

CHROMIUM Cr 1857°C

IRON Fe 1535°C

CARBON C 3550°C

HEAT + SERVE

Drawson's GUMBO

3 bacon slices, quartered
½ green pepper, sliced
½ red " "
1 Spanish onion, diced
1 or 2 garlic cloves, crushed
1 bay leaf
1½ cups fish stock
(or clam juice)
salt, pepper, & thyme to taste
dash cayenne pepper

16 oz. can plum tomatoes
1 tablespoon flour
3 or 4 Italian spicy sausages, quartered
6 or 7 okras, sliced
¼ cup red wine
1 lb. raw prawns in shells
1 pint oysters, shucked
½ lb. scallops
3 crab legs, halved

In large enamel pot, fry bacon. Add onions, peppers, & garlic & cook until golden. Add sausages & cook until brown. Add wine & tomatoes & let simmer for 10 minutes. Add stock, okra & seasoning & cook 30 minutes at moderate heat. Add crab & prawns & cook for 5 minutes only, adding oysters at very last minute. This will feed Serve immediately over long-grain rice. 6 people.

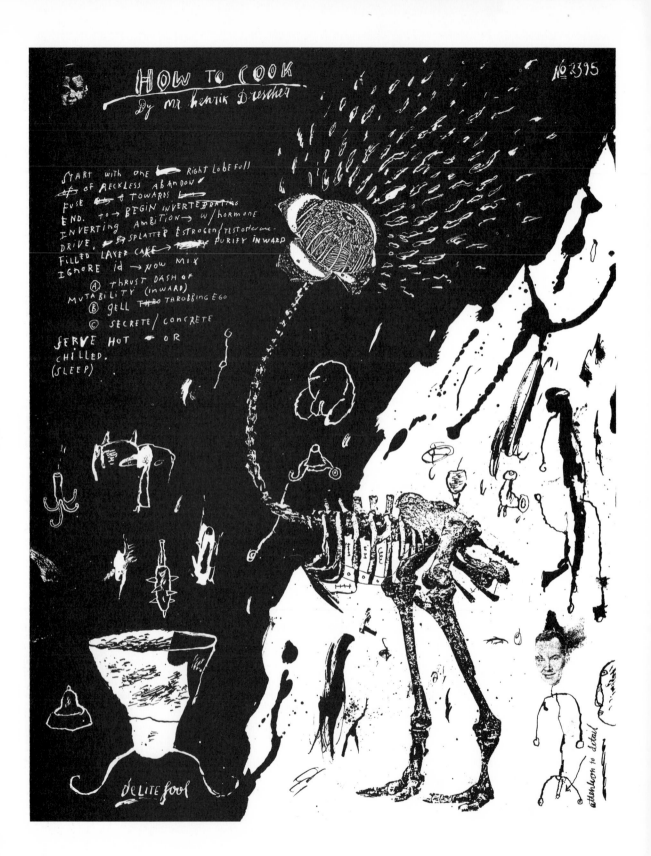

HOW TO COOK
By Mr. Henrik Drescher

START WITH ONE — RIGHT LOBEFULL
of RECKLESS ABANDON
FUSE — TOWARDS
END. TO → BEGIN INVERTEBRATING
INVERTING AMBITION → w/ HORMONE
DRIVE, — SPLATTER ESTROGEN/TESTOSTERONE
FILLED LAYER CAKE → PURIFY INWARD
IGNORE id → NOW MIX
   Ⓐ THRUST DASH OF
MUTABILITY (INWARD)
   Ⓑ GELL THRU THROBBING EGO
   Ⓒ SECRETE / CONCRETE

SERVE HOT — OR
CHILLED.
(SLEEP)

DELITE fool

attention to detail

PORTUGUESE BASEBALL SOUP

(KALE SOUP—NEW BEDFORD STYLE)

INGREDIENTS: ONE LARGE BUNCH OF KALE—½ HEAD OF CABBAGE ABOUT FOUR POUNDS OF SOUP CHUCK WITH BONE—ONE LARGE ONE POUND OF CHOURICO AND ONE POUND OF LINGUICA CLOVE (PORTUGUESE SAUSAGES) CUT THEM INTO 3 INCH PIECES OF ONE LARGE ONE PACKAGE OF LIMA GARLIC ONION. BEANS—ONE CAN RED KIDNEY BEANS— ABOUT TEN BASEBALL-SIZED POTATOES—

KALE IA BRANCO

PUT CHUCK IN VERY LARGE SOUP POT AND COVER GENEROUSLY WITH WATER. ADD LARGE SLICES OF ONION, CLOVE OF GARLIC AND BRING TO BOIL. PUT ON LOW HEAT AND SIMMER WHILE COVERED. IN ANOTHER POT PUT IN LINGUICA AND CHOURICO. COVER WITH WATER AND BRING TO BOIL. SIMMER MEAT AND SAUSAGES FOR ½ HOUR OR UNTIL TENDER. TRIM THE LEAFY PARTS OF KALE AND DISCARD THE TOUGH STEMS. WASH THOROUGHLY AND CHOP COURSLY. DIVIDE CABBAGE INTO LARGE CHUNKS REMOV- ING STEM. WASH AND PEEL POTATOES. DRAIN AND WASH KIDNEY AND LIMA BEANS. BOIL POTATOES SEPERATELY FOR FIFTEEN MINUTES. SKIM FAT FROM SAUSAGE POT. TAKE TENDER SOUP CHUCK OUT OF POT. REMOVE BONE AND KEEP ASIDE. ADD KALE, CABBAGE AND LIMA BEANS TO COM- BINED SAUSAGE AND MEAT BROTH. SIMMER UNTIL KALE IS TENDER (APPROX. 20 MIN.) ADD POTATOES AND BROTH (POTATOES CAN BE WHOLE OR CUT UP) AND KIDNEY BEANS AND MEAT. LET SIMMER FOR ANOTHER FIVE TO TEN MINUTES. REMOVE TWO POTATOES—MASH THEM UP AND ADD THEM TO BROTH FOR THICKENING. TASTES BEST WHEN ALLOWED TO STEEP FOR A DAY OR TWO.

ENOS

Randall Enos

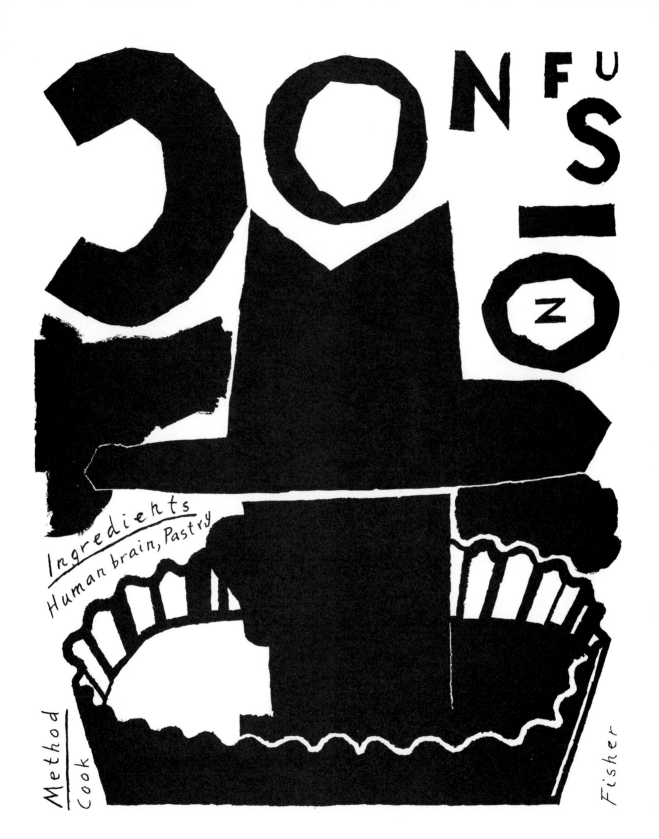

Jeffrey Fisher

Thai Iced Coffee

Place 3 tablespoons of sweetened condensed milk in a tall glass

fill the glass with ice cubes

pour hot + strong coffee
from Sumatra into the glass

Vivienne
Flesher

Douglas Fraser

GORECIPE

① PUT 40 OUNCES OF whiskey IN A Large TUMBLER

② add 1 ICE CUBE

③ PUT IN 2 DROPS OF turpentine

④ ADD AN Egg

⑤ Shake Vigorously And Swallow in one gulp.

THIS RECIPE CAME TO ME IN A VISION ON JUNE 6, 1974 7:26 A.M. WITH THE DIVINE INSPIRATION OF BUFFALO BILL CODY, NAPOLEON AND SUPERFLY

Josh Gosfield

Strawberry Cream Twinkies™

DE-LITE-FULL • makes-a-mess

BY RODNEY A. GREENBLAT (artist)

Yum Yum! cream filled gooey pink fun!

GLOPPY

makes 8 servings

2 cups of COTTAGE CHEESE

1 cup of PLAIN YOGURT

3 TABLESPOONS of HONEY

3 TABLESPOONS of Lemon JUICE

2 CUPS OF STRAWBERRIES, Hulled, Washed and patted dry.

8 HOSTESS TWINKIES

BZZZZ RRRrrrr wmmmm

Place cottage cheese in a food processor and process until smooth. Add the yogurt, honey, lemon juice and strawberries and process untill pureed. Pour over twinkies and chill for several hours before serving.

for even more fun, TOP with A Generous BLOB OF WHIPPED CREAM AND sprinkles!
✳ ♡ ◎ ⊠ ♧ ⫽⫽⫽

CHOMP CHOMP

Lick Slurp SLURP

GLUNK GLUNK

DIG IN!

RG 1992

Ital-Yen

Yellowtail in a nori manicotti handroll with sun-dried ginger in extra virgin rice-bran oil and balsamic tamari with grated aged tofu.

Jessie's
"Nut Yum Yums"

½ pound of butter
4 tablespoons of xxx confectioners sugar
2 cups of flour
1 teaspoon of vanilla
1 tablespoon of cold water
2 cups 'o NUTS

Cream all of the above ingredients together. Roll like a date and drop onto an ungreased cookie sheet. Bake in a slow oven at 250° for about an hour. ('til golden brown) While they are still warm, roll them in more XXX sugar.

4 food groups

Nut salad
Nut Yum Yums
Nut bread
Nut meats

RABBIT STEW

FIRST → YOU MUST CATCH YOUR RABBIT

William Joyce's Recipe for:

ONE ENCHANTED EVENING

INGREDIENTS: TWO LIKE MINDED SOULS:
Should have knowledge of tripping the light fantastic. Must have gone to the moon on gossamer wings at least once. Should be able to face the music while dancing.
MOONLIGHT:
Nocturnal illumination essential, full moon preferred, though silvery moons and blue moons (especially in Kentucky) will suffice.
LOVE SONGS:
Should have plaintive, soothing melodies with that all important dash of heartbreak. Gershwin recommended though almost anything from that era will do. Nonsense songs (Yes, We Have No Bananas, Three Little Fishes, Silly Pie) are recommended for the eccentric and excessively giddy. Avoid Heavy Metal at all costs.
NECTAR OF THE GODS:
Martinis or champagne recommended. Be warned-wines, especially domestic ones, can turn enchantment into tofu-like substance. Beer is simply too tawdry and should be used in cases of glandular emergency only.
ANTI-GRAVITY DEVICE:
For genuine enchantment to congeal, a dollop of whimsey is necessary. This should do the trick.

I CANT COOK

YOU BET
SHE CAN'T

BUT IF YOU WANT TO MAKE A HOT
LEMONADE WHEN YOU ARE SICK MAKE
SURE YOU PEEL THE LEMON BEFORE YOU
SLICE IT AND BE SURE TO SPIT OUT SPIT OUT
THE PITS. MAIRA
KALMAN

Señor Quick Bob's Party Salsa

FAST · EASY · DELICIOUS!

- 1 JAR ORTEGA® MILD SALSA
- 1 JAR ORTEGA® MEDIUM SALSA—
  OR 2 CANS EITHER EMBASSA OR
  HERDEZ SALSA, IF AVAILABLE
- 3/4 CUP FINELY CHOPPED
  GREEN ONIONS
- 1/3 – 1/2 CUP FINELY CHOPPED
  CILANTRO (TO TASTE)
- 3–4 MEDIUM TOMATOES, CHOPPED

MIX WELL AND
REFRIGERATE 2–3 HOURS
SERVE WITH TORTILLA CHIPS, OR
FRITO'S® KING SIZE DIP CHIPS
—Y CERVEZA BUEN FRIA!

MY PROBLEMS — A HEARTY STEW

SERVES: AS MANY AS WILL LISTEN
INTO A POT OF HEAVY SENSIBILITY.

ADD — 5 LBS TENDER CUTS OF FAILURE
DASHED HOPES AND SOURED DREAMS
— 1 TSP OF SELF-ESTEEM (NON-RISING)

— 65 FINELY SELECTED   PAINFUL
CHILDHOOD MEMORIES   (NON-DISSOLVING).
— 2 TOXIC PARENTS.
4 FAILED RELATIONSHIPS.   1 DIVORCE,
POUR ALL THIS INTO 19 GALLONS   OF TEARS,
COVER WITH   SIGHS,
SIMMER FOR 25   YEARS,
BRINGING TO A BOIL   FREQUENTLY.

ENJOY

KOREN

Ed Koren

RECIPE FOR A RIOT

This recipe comes from Decades of Rage

44 Servings more than 1,765 injured — 198 critically

Add: a deadly mixture of ½ cup police officer's *Racism* 56 baton swings, ½ lb. skinned *Rodney King* 81- slices canned amateur videotape

Combine with: *Policemen Acquitted in Taped Beating* Stumbling Economy Uzi semi-automatic violence, Poverty, drugs, bad schools, racial tension:

Bake the dish in a hot LOS ANGELES oven for about two days nearly unchecked *React Slowly as Violence Spreads* Serve it with: 5,000 Federal troops *pleads for peace* **a wake-up call to the rest of America**

© PETER KUPER

Chicken Breasts Hawaiian

2 chicken breasts
1 egg, slightly beaten
1 cup finely grated
bread crumbs
1 tsp. salt
1 cup pineapple juice
2 tbsp. lemon juice
1 tbsp. cornstarch
¼ tsp. curry paste
1 tbsp. sugar
slivered almonds

Split breasts in half. Remove bones, keeping meat in one piece. Dip in egg. Roll in bread crumbs. Season with salt. Pan fry in ¼ inch hot fat in a heavy skillet until brown. Remove fat from pan. Combine juices, cornstarch, curry, and sugar. Pour over chicken. Cover skillet and cook slowly for 20 to 25 minutes. Top with slivered almonds. Serves 4.

Anita Kunz

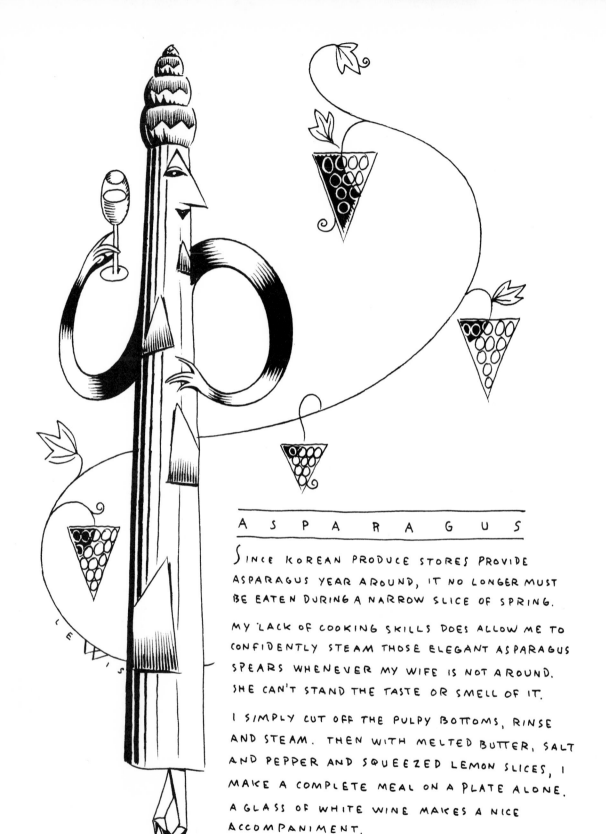

A S P A R A G U S

Since Korean produce stores provide asparagus year around, it no longer must be eaten during a narrow slice of spring.

My lack of cooking skills does allow me to confidently steam those elegant asparagus spears whenever my wife is not around. She can't stand the taste or smell of it.

I simply cut off the pulpy bottoms, rinse and steam. Then with melted butter, salt and pepper and squeezed lemon slices, I make a complete meal on a plate alone. A glass of white wine makes a nice accompaniment.

Angel food cake
Sift 1¼ cup sugar two times. Sift ¼ of this with 1 cup of flour. Sift again and then a third time, this time with ½ teaspoon salt.

ip ab gg whites tablespo and 1 ta nl ... em until fo a 1 teaspoon tartar to until egg w stiff and in ¼ teaspoon illa and ½ tea

Now, wh out 1 e and one an H_2O blespoo on juice my. Add cream of this. Whip hites are then fold van spa

on almond extract. Gradually whip in the rest of the sugar. Pour all of it in to a tube pan and bake 45 minutes at $350°$. L

RECIPE: CHILLIN' HOBO STEW, SERVES 40

SOAK FIVE POUNDS PINTO BEANS OVERNIGHT. COOK BEANS IN ONE AND A HALF GALLONS OF WATER OVER MEDIUM HEAT UNTIL ALMOST SOFT. DICE THREE ONIONS AND THREE RED AND THREE GREEN PEPPERS. CHOP HANDFUL FRESH GINGER, HANDFUL GARLIC AND ONE LONG HOT PEPPER INCLUDING SEEDS. COVER BOTTOM OF POT WITH OLIVE OIL, BRING TO HIGH HEAT, ADD ALL INGREDIENTS AND SAUTÉ. WHEN LIGHT BROWN, ADD CUPS OF WATER, STIRRING TILL LIQUID COVERS ALL. SALT AND PEPPER TO TASTE. ADD CHUNKS OF BUTTERNUT SQUASH AND CUBES OF DAY-OLD BLACK BREAD WITH RAISINS. STIR TILL BREAD IS SOGGY. MARRY MIXTURE WITH BEANS AND STIR OVER MEDIUM HEAT TILL BEANS START TO THICKEN. SERVE WITH SLICES OF FRESH LEMON.

Stan Mack

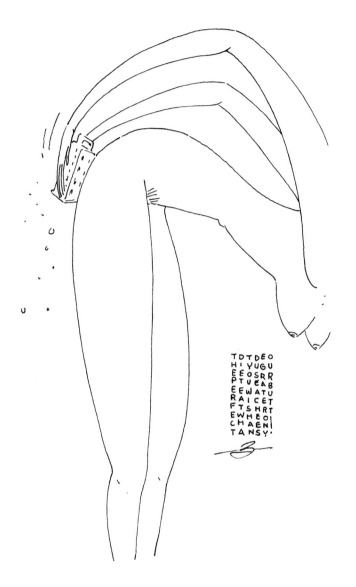

RECIPE FOR WAH-LAH!

RECIPE FROM 'CHEZ CHAZ' ©1990 by PATRICK McDONNELL

David McLimans

Kimble's
Brooklyn Beer Cole Slaw

1 head red cabbage
1/2 red spanish onion
1 cup mayonaise
1 12 ounce bottle of beer
(brooklyn or otherwise)
1/2 cup golden raisins
...

Slice cabbage and onion thinly. In a large bowl add mayonaise, raisins and 1/2 of the beer. (Enjoy the rest yourself.)
Mix well. Garnish with black pepper. Chill!
(Add grated carrot or red bell pepper for color)

RECIPE FOR SUCCESS

BY P. MEISEL

1. One pound of pluck.

2. A sprig of verve.

3. One clump of gumption.

4. One small can of grit.

5. A bucketful of guts.

6. Serve.

Paul Meisel

My brother's BBQ'd Fish dish
Clean and scale ..... fish —
Brush .... olive
oil, g..... .... or cilantro
and salt & pepper. Line the
body .... salt & lemon
juic..... .... once,
cook about .... 1"
thick fish. If you wish
add a dab ....
mixed .... juice,
musi....., ground pepper &
parsley. When done. Serve
hot and make often. munck

HOW TO SEPARATE AN EGG
OR
WHO IS MY MOTHER ?

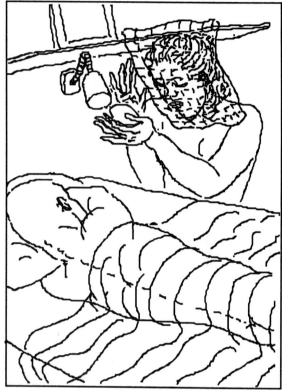

Ingredients
•
3 women
2 men
1 dish
$10,000 in cash

• Take woman #1 and carefully separate the egg and remove from her ovaries. Store in sterile place.

• Have man #1 ejaculate into a test tube and refrigerate sperm until ready to use. (These steps may be done at any time.)

note - make sure you accurately record man and woman's IQ, race, religion, color of hair, eyes, skin, height, weight and size of nose and feet. This information must be readily available upon request.
important - The identity of the man #1 and the woman #1 must be kept secret and properly sealed and protected.

• Place egg and sperm in dish and watch carefully. You will see the sperm gravitate towards the egg and "fertilize" it.
note - some recipes refer to this step as the "miracle of life".

• Take woman #2 and prepare her to receive the fertilized egg. When ready gently place the egg into her womb. Her abdomen will rise very slowly (set timer) for 9 months.
note - you may have seen this referred to as "bun in the oven" in other recipes.

• With woman #2 in proper position (on back with legs apart and up) the egg will have transformed into a baby and with some tugging and pulling the baby will pop out of the "oven".

• Clean and dress baby and place in the arms of woman #3 with man #2 by her side.

• Collect $10,000 and distribute appropriately.

• QUIZ QUESTION •
Who is the mother?

© 1992 Barbara Nessim

Barbara Nessim

RECYCLED SEX WAX MUFFINS

BY "BARNEY" NEUBECKER "FLIPPER" BACON (CONSULT.)

1. WHAT DO YOU DO WITH THOSE MISSHAPPEN SAND ENCRUSTED SEX WAX NUBBINS?

FIG 2. DOUBLE BOIL OVER MEDIUM HEAT. WAX WILL LIQUIFY & SAND & CRUD SINK TO BOTTOM OF PAN.

SEA SPRITE AMANDA

3. POUR INTO TEFLON MUFFIN PAN. CAREFUL TO LEAVE SAND IN BOTTOM.

SAND

STEP 4. WHEN WAX HARDENS CAKES WILL SHRINK & PULL AWAY FROM MUFFIN TIN. POP OUT & GO SURF.

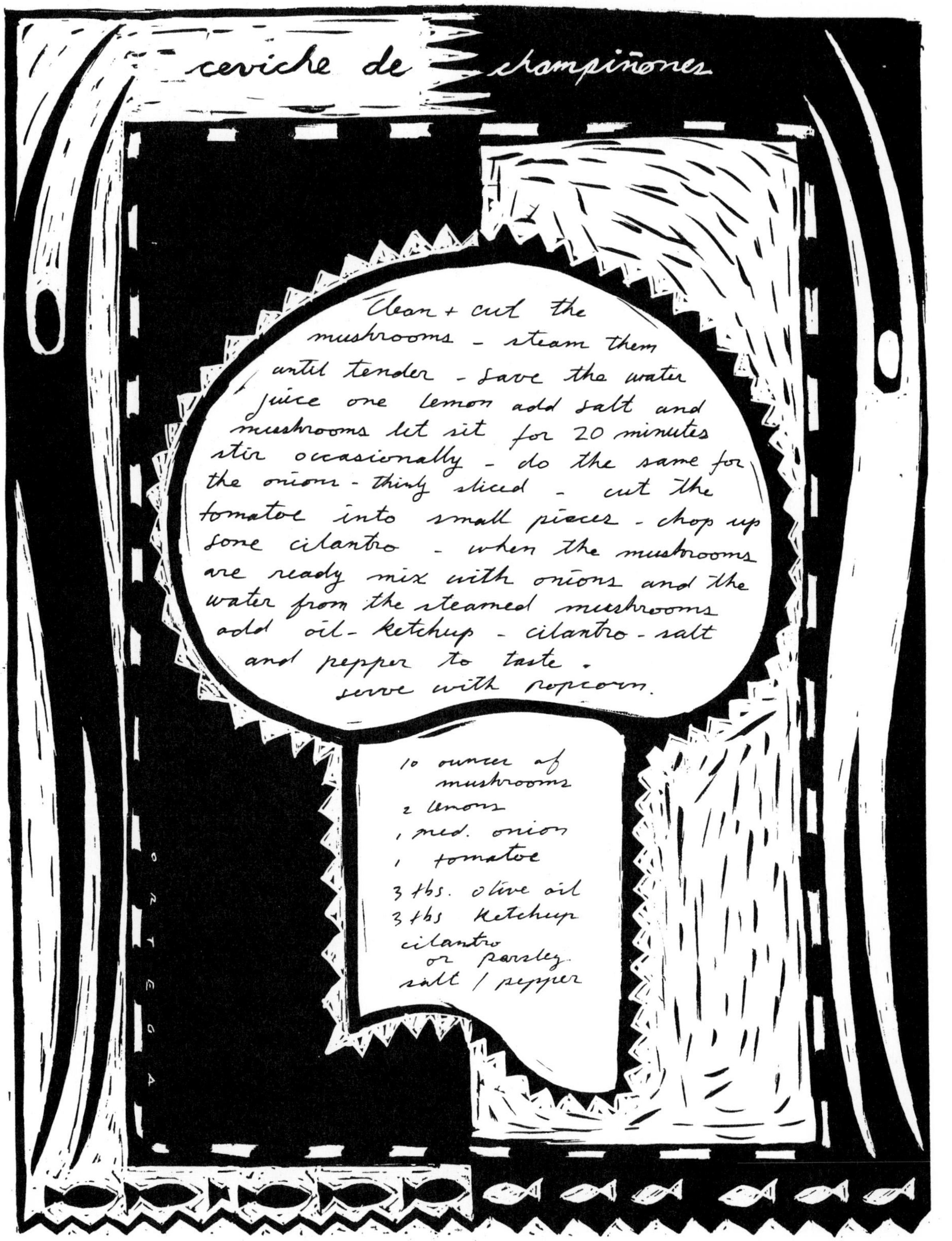

ceviche de champiñones

Clean + cut the mushrooms – steam them until tender – save the water juice one lemon add salt and mushrooms let sit for 20 minutes stir occasionally – do the same for the onions – thinly sliced – cut the tomatoe into small pieces – chop up some cilantro – when the mushrooms are ready mix with onions and the water from the steamed mushrooms add oil – ketchup – cilantro – salt and pepper to taste.
serve with popcorn.

10 ounces of mushrooms
2 lemons
1 med. onion
1 tomatoe
3 tbs. olive oil
3 tbs ketchup
cilantro or parsley
salt / pepper

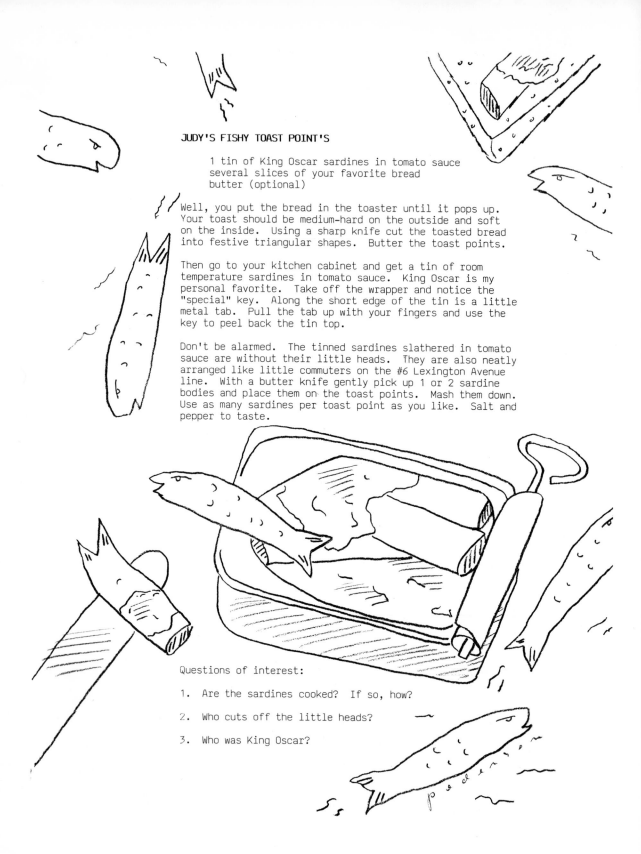

JUDY'S FISHY TOAST POINT'S

1 tin of King Oscar sardines in tomato sauce
several slices of your favorite bread
butter (optional)

Well, you put the bread in the toaster until it pops up.
Your toast should be medium-hard on the outside and soft
on the inside. Using a sharp knife cut the toasted bread
into festive triangular shapes. Butter the toast points.

Then go to your kitchen cabinet and get a tin of room
temperature sardines in tomato sauce. King Oscar is my
personal favorite. Take off the wrapper and notice the
"special" key. Along the short edge of the tin is a little
metal tab. Pull the tab up with your fingers and use the
key to peel back the tin top.

Don't be alarmed. The tinned sardines slathered in tomato
sauce are without their little heads. They are also neatly
arranged like little commuters on the #6 Lexington Avenue
line. With a butter knife gently pick up 1 or 2 sardine
bodies and place them on the toast points. Mash them down.
Use as many sardines per toast point as you like. Salt and
pepper to taste.

Questions of interest:

1. Are the sardines cooked? If so, how?

2. Who cuts off the little heads?

3. Who was King Oscar?

Judy Pedersen

~A GUIDE TO AN UNFORGETTABLE EVENING AT A PARISIAN RESTAURANT~

DÎNER CHEZ ANDRÉ

PEER IN _ MEET THE MAÎTRE D' AND HIS POLITE SMILE

HAVE A SEAT. THE ONLY AVAILABLE TABLE IS THE ONE JUST BESIDE THE REVOLVING DOOR

KEEP COOL. IT MIGHT TAKE SOME TIME TO GET THE WAITER'S ATTENTION

WAIT ABOUT AN HOUR FOR YOUR HORS D'OEUVRE

HURRY UP. PEOPLE ARE WAITING FOR YOUR TABLE

TOTALLY OVERPRICED? MAYBE, BUT THIS IS PARIS AND, AS SAYS ANDRÉ, "AU REVOIR ET À BIENTÔT!"

petit-roulet

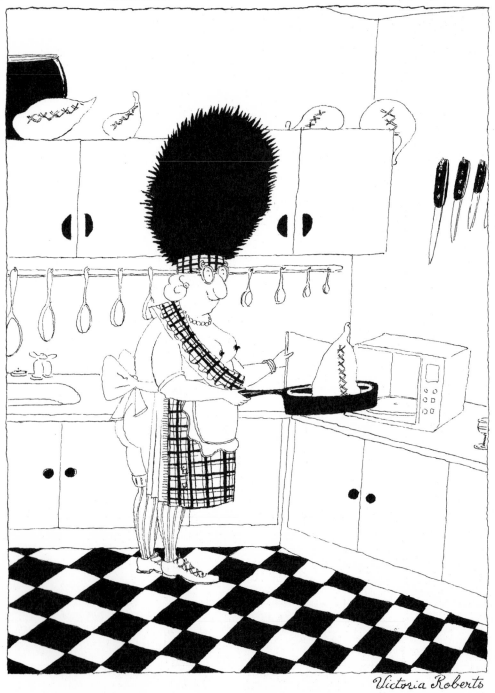

SIMMER DOWN. DON'T BOIL OVER. SIFT. CHILL.

Recipe for
The proper way to
Take A BATH.

2. 1. Get favorite
Run the bath. robe and
Add bath salts. slippers.

Violette

3. MEANWhile,
Make a cup of hot
tea.

4. Light · PEppermint
candles. to increase circu- la- tion.

· Chamomile to relax

5. Put on Il Trovatore or Moonlight Sonata.
6. Cat comes in.

Rogers

Lilla Rogers

71

RECIPE FOR SUCCESS AS AN ACOUSTIC REACTIONARY.

1. TO INSURE MASS MARKET ACCEPTANCE, HIRE SEASONED (22 YEAR OLD) PRODUCT MANAGERS TO CONVERT YOUR MUSIC INTO A DRUG. REMEMBER: HORMONES = PROFITS. NO TALENT INVOLVED.

2. CALL YOURSELF THE 'SOCIAL LUBRICANT-ONE-MAN-MARCHING BAND'. NEVER APPEAR IN PUBLIC. LYRICS AS FOUL AS POSSIBLE... WEAR LOTS OF COSMETIC DIRT. SNEER.

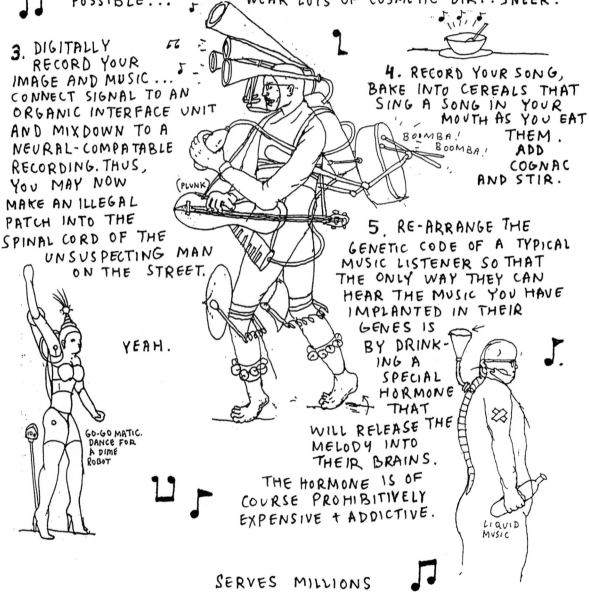

3. DIGITALLY RECORD YOUR IMAGE AND MUSIC... CONNECT SIGNAL TO AN ORGANIC INTERFACE UNIT AND MIXDOWN TO A NEURAL-COMPATABLE RECORDING. THUS, YOU MAY NOW MAKE AN ILLEGAL PATCH INTO THE SPINAL CORD OF THE UNSUSPECTING MAN ON THE STREET.

(PLUNK)

4. RECORD YOUR SONG, BAKE INTO CEREALS THAT SING A SONG IN YOUR MOUTH AS YOU EAT THEM. ADD COGNAC AND STIR.

BOOMBA! BOOMBA!

5. RE-ARRANGE THE GENETIC CODE OF A TYPICAL MUSIC LISTENER SO THAT THE ONLY WAY THEY CAN HEAR THE MUSIC YOU HAVE IMPLANTED IN THEIR GENES IS BY DRINKING A SPECIAL HORMONE THAT WILL RELEASE THE MELODY INTO THEIR BRAINS. THE HORMONE IS OF COURSE PROHIBITIVELY EXPENSIVE + ADDICTIVE.

YEAH.

GO-GO MATIC. DANCE FOR A DIME ROBOT

10¢

LIQUID MUSIC

SERVES MILLIONS

JONATHON ROSEN

playdoh

Marc Rosenthal

THE HOLY ✝ GRUEL

YOU WILL NEED: 1/3 CUP ROLLED OATS, A PINCH OF SALT, 3/4 CUP WATER ∴ BOIL WATER + SALT IN COVERED POT ∴ STIR IN THE OATS ∴ RETURN TO A BOIL ∴ REDUCE HEAT, CONTINUING TO BOIL ∴ COOK UNCOVERED ABOUT 5 MINUTES, STIRRING NOW + THEN ∴ REMOVE FROM HEAT ∴ SERVE THE GRUEL IN AN ORNATE, CUP-LIKE DISH ∴ ADD MILK, HONEY, CINNAMON + BUTTER TO TASTE ∴ OR MAPLE SYRUP INSTEAD OF HONEY ∴ MMM ∴ ENJOY, FOR IT IS GOOD AND COMELY FOR ONE TO EAT ... AND ENJOY THE GOOD OF ALL HIS (OR HER) LABOR ∥ ECCL 5:18

BISCOTTI

4 oz BLANCHED ALMONDS
2½ c flour
¾ c Sugar
3 large eggs

pinch of SALT
3 oz. semi sweet chocolate morsels
1 lg. egg white

375° OVEN

BAKE ALMONDS until golden (20 min)
Finely grind ⅓ & Coarsely grind remaining Almonds
Put flour on BOARD ON A MOUND + MAKE A Well IN the
center. Put All the Almonds, Sugar, EGGS, SALT + baking soda
IN well. MIX All ingred. together, then start to incorporate
the flour until All but 2 tbd. have been INCORP.. KNEAD FOR
2 min then ADD choc pieces kneading them into the dough
Along with the remaining flour. lightly butter + flour A
BAKING sheet. — DIVIDE DOUGH INTO 4 PIECES. SHAPE INTO
A long roll (½" diA.) PLACE rolls on the baking sheet, BEAT
Egg white slightly + brush tops of rolls, BAKE 20 MIN —
REMOVE rolls from oven + with a long knife cut A 45° Angle
(diagonally every ½") RETURN Biscotti to 225° OVEN +
BAKE 30 MIN. REMOVE + cool

FRIED PEANUT BUTTER AND BANANA SANDWICHES

Spread two pieces of Wonder Bread with chunky style peanut butter,

place thinly sliced bananas in center, seal shut, and slather

the outsides with margarine. Fry in heavy skillet. Elvis still can't stop eatin' em,

I. Samaras '92

Isabel Samaras

77

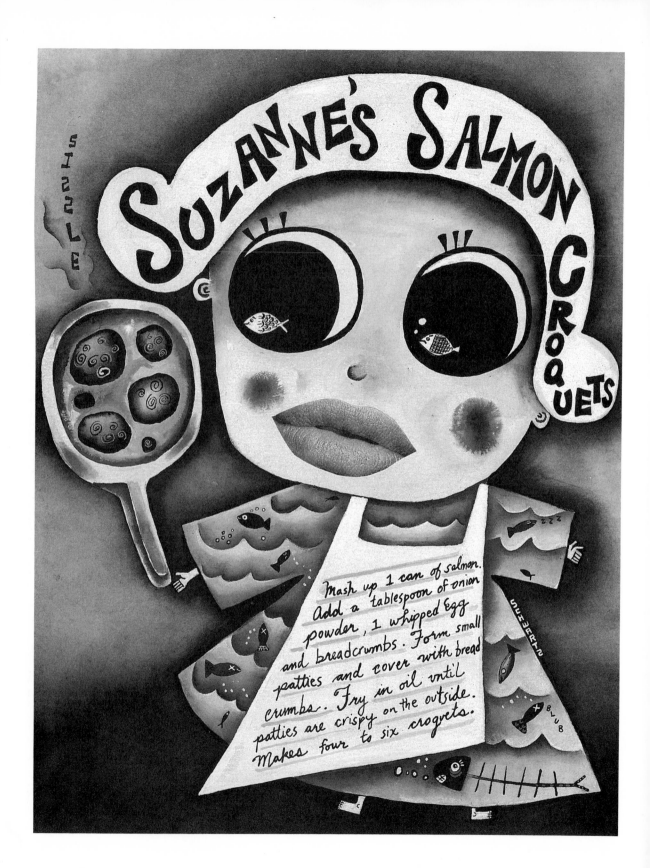

CALM
BALM

(to still attacks of panic, anxiety, stress, and night terrors)
... For this version: ...

Summon a trusted loved one;
Stand or recline;
Move close ... be still.
Add human touch: have
 them lay hands on you.
Embrace.
Add neither fondle nor kiss;
Be still ...

...feel warmth rise...

Breathe;
Break silences... cry if
 you must.
Let warm breath and whispers
 into your ear.
Pass such to beloved other.
Be still, still... breathe.
Repeat all, till calm.
(Holding time will vary.)

Tom Sciacca

79

Michael Sloan

Once I invited my High School pal, Jon Wong, for some of Mom's home-cooking. It was February and she served up my favorite winter dish, a hot, steamy, tangy **KAPUSNIAK** a soup recipe from the Old Country that makes those Campbells Hearty "Man-Pleasers" seem like limp-wristed sissy-water by comparison.

Jon looked dubiously at the savory bowl and gingerly tried a tentative half-spoonful of the indescribable sweet-and-sour broth. His mouth puckered to a tiny asterisk as if he'd swallowed a live frog. For five minutes he made soft, quick panting sounds while the Spiegelman family happily slurped through several helpings.

Jon finally found his voice and hoarsely whispered: "I can't believe it - Jews eat SAUERKRAUT soup!"

He refused to try another drop, or even **try** the CHULENT stew that Mom made as the main dish.... I guess he thought it was made with dead babies.

ONCE I invited my High School pal, Jon Wong, for some of Mom's home-cooking!

KAPUSNIAK- 6-8 servings

- 1 pound of sauerkraut, canned or fresh, the more sour the better.
- 2 pounds Flanken, or short ribs.
- ½ cup brown sugar.
- 2 crushed cloves of garlic
- 1 pound canned tomatoes
- 4 cups of water.

Place everything into a 5 quart kettle and simmer for 2-2½ hours, stirring frequently, until the meat is tender. Remove meat, then skim fat off soup. (If possible, refrigerate overnight, then remove congealed fat.)

Cut meat into bite-size pieces and re-place into soup. Reheat and serve.

PUMPKIN CARAMEL CUSTARD

BRUSH YOUR MEAT OR POTATOES OR FISH WITH SPRY BEFORE BAKIN' OR BROILIN'. THEY'LL HAVE BETTER FLAVOR — WON'T DRY OUT

NANCY STAHL

cook 2/3 c. sugar and 1/4 c. water in a heavy saucepan until sugar dissolves - increase heat and boil without stirring until color becomes a deep caramel - pour into bottom of six individual souffle dishes - set aside at room temperature - in a heavy medium-sized saucepan over medium heat stir 1 3/4 c. cream, 1 1/4 c. canned pumpkin, 1/2 t. cinnamon, 1/8 t. cloves, and a pinch of nutmeg until lukewarm - with an electric mixer beat 4 large egg yolks and 2 whole eggs in a large bowl - gradually add 1 1/2 c. sugar - add the pumpkin mixture and beat until just blended - pour into souffle dishes - place in a large deep baking pan - add enough water to come up halfway on side of dishes - bake until a knife inserted in the centers comes clean (about 1 hour) - cool on a rack for 1 hour - worth the calories - refrigerate at least 4 hours

preheat oven to 350

PARIS

Paris Rolls.

One quart of flour,
two eggs,
one tablespoon of lard,
teaspoon of salt,
half teacup of hop yeast.

Mix at night,

knead thoroughly in the morning,

and bake when light.

ROLLS

Sally Mara Sturman

~Curry Potato Salad~

6 medium potatoes
1 red pepper
3 stalks green onion
1/3 cup curry powder
1 cup mayonnaise
fresh dill

Boil the potatoes. Cool them under cold water. Chop the green onions and red pepper. Cut the potatoes into manageable sections. Mix the curry and mayonnaise. Mix all the ingredients in a bowl. Sprinkle with fresh chopped dill. Serves 6.

Nice at any time of the year.

Maurice Vellekoop 1992

Philippe Weisbecker

BIOGRAPHIES

LISA ADAMS grew up in Northern Vermont and now lives and works in Tribeca, in New York City. Her illustrations, which are an unusual combination of black-and-white and color elements, are commissioned for many books, magazines, and ad campaigns.

MACIEK ALBRECHT, in addition to illustrating full-time, founded Fabrika Studio in 1990, where he produces animated shorts, acting as both director and art director. Prior to establishing his own studio, Mr. Albrecht did animation with The Ink Tank and Colossal Studios, working on many award-winning projects. In recent years, Mr. Albrecht has been dividing his time between New York City and Poland.

ROBERT CLYDE ANDERSON'S illustrations have appeared in magazines as diverse as *Vogue* and *Pansy Beat*, and he created, with John Epperson, the Lypsinka Coloring Book.

KAREN BARBOUR, originally from San Francisco, has recently married and returned to the area after living in New York City for many years. Her rich and vibrant gouache paintings have been exhibited on both coasts and in Tokyo. Ms. Barbour has illustrated four books for children: *Little Nino's Pizzeria*, *Flamboyan*, *Nancy*, and *Mr. Bowtie*.

CHARLES BARSOTTI lives in Kansas City where he draws cartoons for The New Yorker and many other publications. He has published five cartoon collections including *A Girl Needs a Little Action*, *Kings Don't Carry Money*, and Charles Barsotti's *Texas*. He is currently working on an extensive packaging design project for W.H. Smith in England.

MICHAEL BARTALOS has collaborated with Purgatory Pie Press on many limited-edition letterpress books, posters, and post cards, examples of which are in museum collections including The Cooper Hewitt Museum, The Metropolitan Museum, The Museum of Modern Art, The New York Public Library Rare Book Collection, The Tate Gallery, and The Victoria & Albert Museum in London. He has done extensive projects in Japan. He is presently exploring the potential of the computer as a tool to interpret his energetic, graphic illustration style.

GARY BASEMAN, not surprisingly, lists Groucho Marx, Elvis Costello, and Saul Steinberg among his influences. Mr. Baseman puts his ubiquitous sketchbook aside long enough to create illustrations for clients including AT&T, Apple Computer, and *Time* magazine, and to do animation for The Ink Tank in New York City. Mr. Baseman divides his time between the east and west coasts.

MELINDA BECK recently executed the first in a planned series of triptychs in collaboration with Purgatory Pie Press in New York City. Ms. Beck has done illustrations for publications including *The New York Times*, *The Washington Post*, and the *Village Voice* since graduating with a BFA from the Rhode Island School of Design in 1989.

JAMIE BENNETT lives and works in Toronto creating award-winning illustrations for book covers, magazines, posters, calendars, and advertising campaigns.

JAMES BENOIT lives in Bruges, Belgium, with his wife and their two daughters. He is passionate about soccer, likes to ride a bicycle, paint in the morning, and make cartoons in the afternoon. His enigmatic, wry work is featured in numerous magazines in France and Belgium, and he is a regular contributor to a number of American periodicals including *The New Yorker*, for which he has done several covers.

GUY BILLOUT was born in Decize, France, and worked as a designer in Parisian advertising agencies for a number of years before coming to New York City to break into illustration. Since 1982, *The Atlantic Monthly* has given Mr. Billout a full page in every other issue to showcase his adroitly rendered visual puns. He has received numerous Gold and Silver awards from The Society of Illustrators and has written and illustrated five children's books, four of which were included in *The New York Times* list of the "Ten Best Children's Books" in the years they were released. Mr. Billout has trekked to Patagonia and Antarctica in search of inspiration.

MARY LYNN BLASUTTA was born and raised in Columbus, Ohio and studied at the Columbus College of Art & Design. A former art director, Ms. Blasutta currently illustrates in an old farmhouse in the Catskill Mountains.

R.O. BLECHMAN pursues a simultaneous career as an illustrator and director of The Ink Tank, a New York City animation studio. His illustrations have appeared in most major magazines and some exceptional ad campaigns and have been exhibited in galleries in New York, Paris, Berlin, and Munich. In 1984 his animated version of Stravinsky's *The Soldier's Tale* appeared on Public Television and won an Emmy Award.

CATHIE BLECK has won many awards for the sinuous scratchboard illustrations she does from her home in the Midwest, which she shares with her husband and their three children.

SUSAN BLUBAUGH, originally from Ohio, now lives and works in New York City. Some of her favorite pursuits, when she is not illustrating, include figure painting, attending the Metropolitan Opera, and experimenting with odd, pumpkin-based recipes which she tests on willing friends.

GEORGE BOOTH, a native of Missouri, has been contributing his irascible cartoons to *The New Yorker* since 1969. He also does animation for television advertising and books for adults and children including *Possum Comes a Knockin'* by Nancy Van Laan, published by Alfred A. Knopf Books for Young Readers.

KEN BROWN is widely known for cartoons inspired by American popular culture, which can be seen on postcards, mugs, T-shirts, wrapping paper, rubber stamps, stationery, limited-edition color silk-screen prints and in a book titled *Notes From the Nervous Breakdown Lane*. Mr. Brown is also an acclaimed photographer, filmmaker and animator. He lives in a former cheese warehouse in the Tribeca district of New York City with his wife and their daughter.

DIANA BRYAN'S exuberant paper cutout illustrations have appeared in countless magazines and newspapers and have been used for posters, greeting cards, and record album covers. Ms. Bryan also teaches, lectures, and writes extensively about business and safety practices in the arts. She has recently created award-winning video and book versions of *The Fisherman's Wife* and *The Monkey People* for Sony/Rabbit Ears and has been commissioned to design a thirty-foot mural for the children's book sections of Waldenbooks' new Basset Book Stores.

DAVE CALVER lives in a 1940s Tudor house in the middle of the woods and has a collection of more than five hundred pairs of salt and pepper shakers and sixty cookie jars. His sensuous colored pencil illustrations have been commissioned for a wide range of projects and are particularly effective as bookcovers. Mr. Calver takes a break from illustration by designing rugs and clocks and by making miniature and oversized chair models.

ROZ CHAST is a New Yorker cartoonist with a devoted, if not cultlike following. She has published seven volumes of her cartoons: *Last Resorts, Unscientific Americans, Parallel Universes, Poems and Songs, Mondo Boxo, The Four Elements,* and *Proof of Life on Earth.* Ms. Chast has exhibited her original work in many solo and group shows, particularly at The Illustration Gallery in recent years.

EVE CHWAST, a native New Yorker living in Greenwich Village, makes handcolored woodblock prints and three-dimensional papier-mache sculptures that have appeared in numerous publications including *Graphis* and *Frankfurter Allegemeine*. She has also illustrated a children's book called *Grandma's Latkes*.

ALAN COBER has received more than three hundred awards for transcendent visual essays on social issues as well as for his corporate illustration. His list of clients includes Exxon, Prudential Bache, ITT, and Digital.

SANTIAGO COHEN was born in Mexico City and now calls Hoboken, New Jersey, his home. In addition to illustrating for a wide variety of magazines and newspapers, Mr. Cohen has designed a number of Christmas cards for The Museum of Modern Art in New York City.

PAUL CORIO has illustrated for the usual publications but has done some of his most interesting work in small, self-published, semi-autobiographical books. He has also played drums on five albums with various bands and was briefly apprenticed to a tattoo artist.

BRIAN CRONIN divides his time between Ireland, his place of birth, and New York City. Mr. Cronin first came to the US on a Kilkenny Design Scholarship and returned on a second one for a five-month apprenticeship to Milton Glaser. His work has been commissioned for the Op-Ed pages of major newspapers here and in Ireland, as well as for the usual range of editorial and corporate clients.

ISABELLE DERVAUX, a native of France, works and travels in the US, Europe, and Japan. Among the most unexpected uses of her fresh, charming characters is cookie packaging designed for a Tokyo confectionery. What Is Your Type? consists of five cookie "personalities," each a different shape (triangular, square, oval, trapezoid, and round) in vividly colored, small matching tins nestled in one big tin.

SANDRA DIONISI, a resident of Toronto, creates graphically powerful gouache paintings that have been featured in dozens of magazines and prestigious annuals in Canada and the United States. She enjoys collecting old playing cards and has a cat named Cosimo d'Medici.

BLAIR DRAWSON, a native of Winnipeg, has recently settled in Toronto with his wife and their two children after living in northern California, Connecticut, and British Columbia over the years. His illustrations have won many awards and his personal work has been shown in Toronto, Paris, New York, and Vancouver.

HENRIK DRESCHER'S work reflects the political and social anxieties of the world as he sees it, yet he has also illustrated fifteen highly successful books for children. Included in his work for children is *No Plain Pets*, from which five originals were purchased by The Library of Congress for their permanent collections. A native of Denmark, Mr. Drescher lives in upstate New York with his wife and their three children.

RANDALL ENOS has been illustrating in a distinctive linoleum-block print style for thirty-six years and has done extensive animation for television commercials and film titles, among other things. (He won a television Award at Cannes for a commercial that the client, an insurance company, never aired because it was too "offbeat.") He teaches at Parsons School of Design and The School of Visual Arts.

BETSY EVERITT, originally from California, recently returned there with her husband and their daughter after a sojourn in New York City. Ms. Everitt has three children's books to her credit: *The Happy Hippopatami*, which she illustrated; *Frida, The Wondercat*; and *Mean Soup*, which she wrote as well. Her work has been exhibited in New York, Los Angeles, and Tokyo.

JEFFREY FISHER was born in Melbourne, Australia, and has returned to live there again after travels that took him to Nepal, Southeast Asia, and London, where he lived and worked for many years. One of his most interesting projects was a series of postage stamps on the history of astronomy, commissioned by the British Royal Mail.

VIVIENNE FLESHER has travelled in the South Pacific, the Far East, the Caribbean, and Europe and recently relocated to northern California from her hometown of New York City. Ms. Flesher's rich, unsentimental pastel drawings have been commissioned and widely exhibited in Europe, the US, and Japan.

DOUGLAS FRASER zoomed to the top of the profession immediately upon completing the MFA program at The School of Visual Arts in 1984. Especially notable are large-scale projects Mr. Fraser has undertaken, including a print and animation campaign for Lowenbraü, billboards for Levi Strauss, and five heroic murals in St. Louis's Powerhouse. Mr. Fraser had his first solo exhibition at The Illustration Gallery in 1989.

DAVID GOLDIN has travelled extensively throughout the Far East, India, and Greece and recently went on one of Outward Bound's most gruelling trips. Mr. Goldin brings fascinating materials back from these journeys to incorporate into his highly coveted personal collages, which were the feature of his first solo show at The Illustration Gallery in 1992. Mr. Goldin is hard at work on his first children's book.

JOSH GOSFIELD has been a carpenter, a door-to-door salesman, and, for a number of years, the art director of *New York* magazine. He creates oil and acrylic paintings, often incorporating quirky trademark lettering, for clients including *Rolling Stone*, *Manner Vogue* (Germany), and *Mirabella*. The department store, Barney's New York, commissioned Mr. Gosfield to design seven display windows for Father's Day, 1992. Each extraordinary, memorabilia-crammed installation was a tribute to fathers of various stripes including "Western Dad," "El Padre Latino," "Dream Dad," and "Blue Collar Dad." The cumulative effect of this show was profoundly moving.

RODNEY ALAN GREENBLAT'S talents surpass mere illustration: he creates his own universe out of sculpture, drawings, paintings, reliefs, computer graphics, and animation. Recently Mr. Greenblat created eighty-five painted wood sculptures for a travelling narrative show called "Land-Ho: The Mythic World of Rodney Alan Greenblat," which was commissioned by the Chrysler Museum in Norfolk, Virginia. His work has been featured in almost twenty solo exhibitions and twice as many group shows, and at galleries and museums including The Whitney and The Museum of Modern Art. Mr. Greenblat has written and illustrated three books for children: *Uncle Wizmo's New Used Car*, *Aunt Ippy's Museum of Junk*, and *Slombo the Gross*. He is currently immersed in the field of computer art.

GENE GREIF, formerly an art director, has been creating his distinctive collage illustrations for national magazines and *Fortune 500* companies since 1984. Examples of his work are in the permanent collections of The Museum of Modern Art, The Smithsonian Institute, and the Pompidou Centre in Paris.

STEVEN GUARNACCIA, a prolific illustrator, writer, and lecturer, fills a unique niche in the field of illustration and design. In addition to editorial and corporate illustration and several book projects, Mr. Guarnaccia is currently designing collections of silver and enamel jewelry, neckties, limited edition rugs, and iron sculptures. Somehow, he also finds time to visit flea markets and antique shops to add to his vast collections of vintage books, toys, and ephemera.

JESSIE HARTLAND lives and works in a loft in New York City's financial district with her husband, their son, and two cats. Her work has appeared in many publications in the United States and in Japan, where it is equally well known. Some of her more rewarding projects have been window installations for Barney's New York, a painted mural for Esprit, and the animated movie trailer for Spaulding Gray's *Monster in a Box*. Her first children's book, *Cat Cut*, was published in 1992.

PAMELA HOBBS, an English illustrator, is one of the new wave of artists exploring the potential of the computer as a design tool. She teaches Computer Graphics in New York city at The School of Visual Arts and The New School for Social Research in New York City. In addition, her work has been written about and exhibited in the United States and Japan.

DAVID JOHNSON, known for elegant and incisive pen & ink portraits in the *New York Times Book Review* and other places, has been concentrating lately on animated video folk tales for

Rabbit Ears Productions. He has done *Thumbelina*, *The Boy Who Drew Cats*, and most recently, *The Bremen Town Musicians*.

WILLIAM JOYCE is the illustrator and author of *George Shrinks*, *Dinosaur Bob and His Adventures With the Family Lazardo*, *Nicholas Cricket*, *A Day With Wilbur Robinson*, *Bently & Egg*, and *Santa Calls*; children's books that became instant prize-winning classics. William Joyce lives in Shreveport, Louisiana, and is at work on a number of film projects including feature-length adaptations of *Nicholas Cricket* and *A Day With Wilbur Robinson*.

MAIRA KALMAN is the author and illustrator of *Hey Willy, See The Pyramids*; *Sayonara, Mrs. Kackleman*; *Max Makes A Million*; *Ooh-la-la, Max In Love*, and most recently, *Max In Hollywood, Baby*. She lives in New York City with her husband and their two children and orders in for dinner.

VICTORIA KANN executes her elegant collages in a small studio surrounded by stacks of old *Popular Mechanics*, obsolete encyclopedias, and obscure medical textbooks. A graduate of the Rhode Island School of Design, Ms. Kann currently lives in New York City, her hometown.

BRUCE ERIC KAPLAN lives in Los Angeles and draws cartoons that appear in *The New Yorker*.

ROBERT KOPECKY was born in San Diego and attended Art Center College of Design in Pasadena. He has worked in animation, publication, and poster design, and as a drawing and illustration teacher at Otis-Parsons in Los Angeles and the Academy of Art in San Francisco. He currently lives in New York City and works as an illustrator and comic artist.

ED KOREN lives in New England and has been contributing cartoons to *The New Yorker* since 1962.

PETER KUPER lives in New York City when not travelling around the world. He is co-editor of the political comic/magazine *World War 3 Illustrated*. The fascinating sketchbook journals he fills in his travels have been published as *ComicsTrips*, which can be found in better comic book shops.

ANITA KUNZ, a native of Toronto, presently divides her time between there and New York City. Since graduating from the Ontario College of Art, Ms. Kunz has created award-winning illustration for books, magazines, and ad campaigns for the Canadian, American, and European markets. Her work has been featured in *Graphis* (Switzerland), *Communication Arts* (US), and *Idea* magazine (Japan).

TIM LEWIS, a native of Michigan, was an illustrator and designer at Push Pin Studio in the 1960s and presently lives in a brown-stone in Brooklyn, where he continues to produce innovative, evolving illustration.

KANDY LITTRELL lives in New York City where she is an art director at *The New York Times Magazine*. She likes to do illustration when the subject interests her and time permits.

STAN MACK'S "Real Life Funnies" in the *Village Voice* and *Adweek's* "Out-Takes" are eagerly awaited long-standing weekly features that capture the essence of the world as Mr. Mack observes it. Whether chronicling the poignant efforts of squatters trying to make an abandoned building into a home or poking gentle fun at the conceits of the advertising world, Mr. Mack's commentary has hit the bull's eye in countless cartoon strips. He is currently working on two fascinating projects: writing and illustrating sophisticated cartoon history books for adults, and collaborating on real-life stories, also in cartoon form, about and for teenagers.

BILL MAYER lives in Atlanta where he produces illustration that has garnered countless awards including Gold and Silver medals from the Society of Illustrators. Some of his most intriguing work can be found between the covers of sketchbooks filled with elegant, extremely lascivious pen-and-ink drawings.

PATRICK McDONNELL lives in New Jersey with his wife and their Jack Russell terrier, Earl. In addition to advertising illustration for clients including AT&T, Nabisco, and Johnson & Johnson, Mr. McDonnell's work has been enjoyed by readers of *Parents* magazine where his "Bad Baby" comic strip has been a monthly feature since 1984, and by readers of *Sports Illustrated*, for whom he does a weekly illustration for the "Scorecard" column. Mr. McDonnell is currently at work turning "Bad Baby" into a prime time television show.

DAVID McLIMANS earned a Master of Fine Arts degree in graphic design from Boston University in 1984 after living abroad for a time in Hong Kong and Vienna. He presently lives in his home state of Wisconsin, where he creates graphic illustration, often incorporating text, for a number of clients including *The Progressive*, *The New York Times*, and The University of Chicago Press.

KIMBLE MEAD grew up in a small New England seaport and has lived in Brooklyn since graduating from Pratt Institute. His illustrations have appeared in many publications and seem especially suited to the pages of *Gourmet* magazine, where his work has appeared for many years.

PAUL MEISEL, in addition to advertising and editorial work, has illustrated many children's books including *Busy Buzzing Bumblebees*, *My World & Globe*, and *Your Insides*. He lives on a road with a funny name in Connecticut with his wife and their three sons.

PAULA MUNCK, a native of Australia, is known for fluid, vibrant gouache paintings which have been commissioned by a stellar list of corporate and editorial clients She has also executed numerous large-scale mural installations in Toronto, where she and her husband have lived for many years. Spending a part of each winter in Jamaica or some other tropical spot, Ms. Munck absorbs the luminous energy evident in her work.

BARBARA NESSIM is one of the foremost proponents of electronic art created on the computer and has lectured and taught widely on the subject. Her paintings and drawings are in the permanent collections of a number of museums, including The Smithsonian Institute, and have been exhibited in galleries worldwide. Ms. Nessim became Chairperson of the Illustration Department at Parsons School of Design in the fall of 1992.

ROBERT NEUBECKER is the illustrator art directors think of when the issue is thorny and the desired approach is penetrating but not heavy-handed. Mr. Neubecker has created award-winning covers for Newsweek, *Global Finance*, and *Time International*, as well as illustration for a broad range of editorial and corporate clients. Based in New York City, Mr. Neubecker likes to travel, especially to places where the surfing or skiing is promising.

JOSÉ ORTEGA, born in Guayaquil, Ecuador, came to New York City when he was five years old. Mr. Ortega began working as an illustrator even before completing the BFA program at the School of Visual Arts in 1986. He cites pre-Columbian, Art Deco, German Expressionist, and comic book art as influences on his work, which has been commissioned by clients including Amnesty International, the *Village Voice*, Nike, and Bloomingdale's. He also collaborated on a magazine prototype called *Gin & Comix*, published under the auspices of SVA.

JUDY PEDERSEN'S distinctive pastel illustrations have graced the covers of at least one hundred books, in addition to a great deal of editorial and corporate projects. She has illustrated three books for children: *The Tiny Patient*, *The Yellow Button*, and *Out In The Country*. Ms. Pedersen has had solo shows of her illustration and personal work at The Illustration Gallery and in Tokyo.

PHILIPPE PETIT-ROULET lives in Paris where he works as a cartoonist and illustrator for many magazines. He has published nine books including two for children. He is presently working on an extensive campaign for a department store in Osaka.

VICTORIA ROBERTS grew up in Mexico City and Sydney, Australia, and now lives in New York City. Her first cartoon strip, "My Sunday," was published in Australia, Holland, and Mexico and compiled into a book released in Australia and Great Britain. Her cartoons and illustrations can be found in *The New Yorker* and *The New York Times*, as well as numerous other publications.

LILLA ROGERS has created lush paintings and pastel drawings, often incorporating her trademark lettering, for more than eighty magazines and countless corporate and publishing clients here and abroad. Ms. Rogers's work has been exhibited and written about extensively in the United States and Japan, where she has had two solo shows. Having lived all over the country and in New York City for a number of years, Ms. Rogers recently settled in the Boston area.

JONATHON ROSEN, a native of California, has lived in New York City since 1985. He studied fine art printmaking for seven years and cites as influences on his mordant work Italian Gothic painting, Flemish illuminated manuscripts, early 20th-century American comic strips, 1950s crime comics, circus art, alchemy engravings, and medical illustration. His work can be seen in *Raw*, *Rolling Stone*, and the *Village Voice* and on projects for Polygram, Arista, and Warner Brothers Records.

MARC ROSENTHAL studied architecture at Princeton University before pursuing his interest in painting and illustration. Mr. Rosenthal worked as a designer with Milton Glaser for five years and currently works and lives in upstate New York with his wife and their son.

JONATHAN ROYCE was born in Moscow (Idaho) and grew up in Puerto Rico. After three years of music school in Boston and a number of years living in Paris, Mr. Royce returned to the States where he divides his time between animation and illustration.

ANTHONY RUSSO is well known for bold scratchboard illustration, as well as for acrylic, watercolor, and oil crayon work, all with a distinctly primitive spirit. His award-winning illustrations are sought after by a wide variety of corporate and editorial clients, and he has done dozens of bookjackets. Mr. Russo lived for a time in Tuscany and has travelled in Thailand, Nepal, England, Germany, Austria, Jamaica, Peru, Iceland, and most recently, Belize, and Costa Rica. He lives in Rhode Island with his wife and their son

RICHARD SALA'S work has appeared in a variety of international comic–strip anthologies, including the critically acclaimed *Raw* magazine, since he graduated with a Masters degree in painting from Mills College. Many of these stories were collected in *Hypnotic Tales*, published by Kitchen Sink Press in 1992. He has written and illustrated a 12-minute, animated pulp-style mystery for MTV's Liquid Television and is at work on another book due to be published in 1993.

ISABEL SAMARAS was Program Director at New York City's Franklin Furnace for three years before she left to pursue her artistic obsession with dead presidents, Japanese monsters, rock personalities, and comic book anti-heroes. Her erotic lunchboxes featuring characters from favorite childhood television shows were first shown at The Illustration Gallery in 1991. Ms. Samaras recently relocated to San Francisco after living in New York City for many years.

SARA SCHWARTZ, a New Yorker and graduate of Pratt Institute, recently completed *A Leaf Named Bud*, a children's book she illustrated and wrote in collaboration with her sister. She is doing more and more illustration in relief constructions of clay, vividly painted with acrylics, often incorporating beads, jewels, and other found objects.

TOM SCIACCA creates his mysterious, lovely paintings in a studio in New York City, where he grew up. Mr. Sciacca worked as a stage actor for a time, both in New York and in London, and has played drums for many years. He currently makes time to study African percussion.

MADDALENA SISTO is an architect who prefers to work as a painter, illustrator, and journalist for such publications as *German Elle, Anna,* and *Casa Vogue* in Italy—magazines in which her work is featured monthly. She writes and illustrates particularly about fashion, design trends, and young international artists. Her work has been exhibited in Stockholm, Tokyo, New York, and many Italian cities including Milan, where she lives. A recent exhibition consisted of a collection of teapots in the shape of women's heads, each with four interchangeable hat-shaped lids.

MICHAEL SLOAN, after graduating from the Rhode Island School of Design, spent several years in France and Italy immersing himself in the classic architecture that he loves and which so clearly informs his work. His training in copper engraving and woodcut printmaking is very apparent in his graphic pen-and-ink work.

ELWOOD H. SMITH was an art director in Chicago for several years before moving to New York City to establish himself in the field of illustration. The artists who have most strongly inspired Mr. Smith are Rube Goldberg, George Herriman ("Krazy Kat"), and Billy DeBeck ("Barney Google"). Mr. Smith lives in a bucolic town in upstate New York with his wife and their numerous cats and dogs.

NANCY SPEIR lives in Sonoma County in northern California with her husband and their horse, dog, and seven cats. She tones down her wildest painting impulses for magazines, greeting cards, and children's books and lets them fly for her personal work, which has appeared in numerous shows at The Illustration Gallery.

ART SPIEGELMAN is a co-founder and editor of *Raw*, the outstanding magazine of avant-garde comics and graphics. Probably best known for *Maus*, a two-volume autobiographical account of growing up as the child of Auschwitz survivors, Mr. Spiegelman is responsible for a singularly moving, almost indescribably powerful work of graphic and narrative art. Original art and working studies from *Maus* were exhibited at The Museum of Modern Art in 1991, and Mr. Spiegelman was awarded a special Pulitzer Prize for the opus in 1992. Mr. Spiegelman currently lives in New York City with his wife and their two children.

NANCY STAHL attended Art Center College in California and the School of Visual Arts in New York City, where she presently lives. Her beautifully designed illustrations have been commissioned for many compact disc covers including a ten-disc Duke Ellington set for Warner Music. Currently exploring the potential of computer graphics, Ms. Stahl plans to do more work in this developing medium.

SALLY MARA STURMAN has travelled to Mexico, Jamaica, and France, where she lived and painted for several years. She presently lives in New York City, where she creates lush colored pencil and oil pastel drawings that are most strikingly used as bookcovers.

MAURICE VELLEKOOP, a native of Toronto, began getting commissions during his third year at the Ontario College of Art, from which he graduated in 1986. His witty, very assured paintings have been honored, exhibited, and published in Canada, the US, and abroad.

PHILIPPE WEISBECKER, born in Dakar, Senegal, was raised in France, where he and his wife now live after twenty-three years in New York City. Followers of Mr. Weisbecker's career have been rewarded by his remarkable and fearless evolution of style. From realistic, intricately crosshatched pen and ink, to flat, deceptively naive drawings watercolored in a childlike palette, Mr. Weisbecker's work has grown primitive and reductive of late. His most recent illustrations are collages made of distressed, unrefined papers highlighted at times with a jagged pen line. His work has been widely exhibited and has won numerous awards.

ROBERT ZIMMERMAN, born and raised in North Carolina, now lives in Brooklyn with his wife and their two children, where he creates graphic, antic illustrations for a wide range of clients.

PAM SOMMERS, a former illustrator, lives in New York City with her husband, Peter Ellers, an advertising executive, and a smooth Fox Terrier named Henry who often accompanies her to the Gallery.